MY FAMILY TREE

NAME: _____

DATE: _____

Royal Horticultural Society

Sharing the best in Gardening

MY FAMILY TREE

JO FOSTER

WHITE LION
PUBLISHING

CONTENTS

All the pages in this notebook are numbered so that notes can be cross-referenced. There is space to add your own contents for the blank pages.

INTRODUCTION
EVERY FAMILY HAS ITS OWN STORIES

Every family has its own stories, which are enormously valuable to discover and share. This notebook is designed to encourage you to write down what you know about your family history, and to give you a structure for the information. There are prompts to spark your memories, and space to write down facts and stories that might otherwise be forgotten, so that you can leave an accessible record for other family members to read. It may also spur you on to find out more – if so, there are tips for getting started in your research at the end of the notebook (see pages 141–7). What you write here will leave a precious record for your relatives to read and enjoy, both now and in the future.

My own grandmother wrote some of her life story in a notebook in her later years, and since her death it has become a valued family heirloom to refer to. There is so much in it that we never talked about, and that I might never have got around to asking. Even if you are close to your relatives, there are many aspects of the past which don't come up in everyday conversation. Writing down or recording what you know, in your own words, will leave a wonderful legacy for the future.

Family history research has become a hugely popular hobby, especially since the growth of online records has made it accessible to more people than ever before. Each researcher may have several different motivations for preserving family stories, and finding out more about their ancestors. For some, the enjoyment and satisfaction of piecing together a puzzle keeps them going. Family history research uses detective skills and creative thinking, as well as methodical searching. Or you may be focused on results: many people feel that knowing about their family tree will bring self-knowledge. You may find you come to understand your own life and character better by reflecting on the ancestors whose experiences and efforts set the scene for their descendants' lives.

Genealogy, the study of family trees and lineages, is a route into a wider interest in history for some. If you follow the threads of your family's story with a curious mind, all sorts of interesting social history and events can open up to you. Studying your ancestors can also lead you into local history, as you find out more about the places where they lived and worked. This can be a fascinating way to explore a new area, or give you a fresh perspective on somewhere you already know.

You may be driven to record your family history mainly for the benefit of future generations, to ensure that the knowledge and memories which have been passed down to you are not lost. Alternatively, you may study the past out of respect for previous generations. For many people, the act of remembering is valuable in itself and can be a form of honouring the people who went before you. It can be important to feel that their lives and struggles are not forgotten. Family history research can also help you to connect with your extended family of living relatives, and to make contact with distant cousins around the world. Whatever your reasons for doing so, this notebook will help you to preserve and uncover your own family's story.

When beginning your family history research, it is important to start with what you know. Your first step in using this notebook is to fill in whatever information you are sure of. If you stop there, it will still have been a useful exercise, but hopefully you will move on to the next step: gathering knowledge from other family members. You could use this book to guide conversations with relatives and fill in the gaps in your knowledge (see interviewing tips, pages 148–51). You can then start to take the story further by doing your own online and archival research (see research tips, pages 142–5).

This notebook encourages you to combine genealogy (researching and assembling your family tree, filling in the names, dates and relationships between people) and family history (adding detail, colour and stories to the basic tree). Towards the front of the book you will find the more structured pages to fill in, starting with family trees and ancestor charts and moving on to profile pages for family groups and individuals.

Don't be concerned if your family doesn't fit into some of the forms in this book. There are blank notes pages at the end which you can use to write down extra information of all sorts, which could include details on additional marriages or adoption records. Families don't often fit neatly into boxes!

Every family has its own shape, especially today as less conventional families are much more common, accepted and celebrated than in the past. Your family may well include divorces and re-marriages, same-sex relationships, single parents or unmarried partners. Use and adapt this notebook to celebrate the family stories that are important to you.

As you fill in this notebook, make a note wherever you can of where you got your information, so that you and others can check it against original documents. Treat all new information with caution until it has been checked; it is especially important not to take for granted the truth of a fact just because it is written down, for instance in someone else's family tree. Now that it is so easy to find and share research online, it is also easier than ever to replicate mistakes. You should distinguish documented facts from memories or rumours, but just as memories can be unreliable, so can documents: it is not unusual for an individual's stated age to vary between their birth, marriage and death records and census entries (see research tips, page 144–5). At the same time, the value of family stories does not lie only in their factual reliability. An unlikely-seeming rumour could have an element of truth, or be a clue to a new discovery. Sometimes the stories, memories and patterns of experience which are handed down through your family can be as important as your genes for shaping your character and future.

FAMILY TREE
MY CLOSE FAMILY

Use the following blank pages to draw a simple tree (in pencil first!) showing you at the centre of your immediate family: this could include your parents, siblings, spouse or partner(s) and child(ren). You will have space to fill in earlier generations on pages that follow. Each box will contain a person's name, date and place of birth, and date and place of death if deceased. Dates and places of marriage can be added between spouses, or in either spouse's box.

Don't expect to start by producing a comprehensive tree – this notebook will help you to build up your tree in sections. You might like to draw out a full tree as you go, but use a large piece of paper and expect to do a fair amount of erasing and re-drawing. There is also a fold-out section on page 132 with space to draw a full tree, once you have progressed with your research. If you would rather work on computer, there are a number of specialist family tree software programs which can help you draw up a tree with any number of relatives on it.

Start by filling in the central box with your own details, then add your parents' details in the boxes above. Add more boxes for other relatives, as shown in the example opposite.

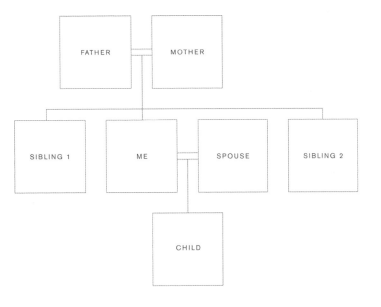

Siblings or other relatives of the same generation should all be on the same horizontal level. Spouses should be in boxes next to each other with a double line joining them. For additional marriages, draw another box on the other side and add the number of the marriage (1/2/3…) above the = sign. Draw a vertical line of descent down from this, with either a box for their only child or a horizontal line to join multiple siblings, drawn in order of age.

FAMILY TREE

MY CLOSE FAMILY

ANCESTOR CHARTS

An ancestor chart, or pedigree chart, is the clearest way to show each generation that came before you. Siblings are not shown – there is space elsewhere in the book for their details. Fill in the information you know about you, your parents and grandparents. If you know about generations further back, you can add them on the following pages.

FATHER
NAME:

DATE & PLACE OF BIRTH:

DATE & PLACE OF DEATH:

ME
NAME:

DATE & PLACE OF BIRTH:

DATE & PLACE OF MARRIAGE:

NAME OF SPOUSE:

DATE & PLACE OF MARRIAGE:

MOTHER
NAME:

DATE & PLACE OF BIRTH:

DATE & PLACE OF DEATH:

GRANDFATHER

NAME:

DATE & PLACE OF BIRTH:

DATE & PLACE OF DEATH:

DATE & PLACE OF MARRIAGE:

GRANDMOTHER

NAME:

DATE & PLACE OF BIRTH:

DATE & PLACE OF DEATH:

GRANDFATHER

NAME:

DATE & PLACE OF BIRTH:

DATE & PLACE OF DEATH:

DATE & PLACE OF MARRIAGE:

GRANDMOTHER

NAME:

DATE & PLACE OF BIRTH:

DATE & PLACE OF DEATH:

ANCESTOR CHARTS

NAME:

DATE & PLACE OF BIRTH:

DATE & PLACE OF DEATH:

PATERNAL GRANDFATHER
NAME:

DATE & PLACE OF BIRTH:

DATE & PLACE OF MARRIAGE:

DATE & PLACE OF DEATH:

DATE & PLACE OF MARRIAGE:

NAME:

DATE & PLACE OF BIRTH:

DATE & PLACE OF DEATH:

NAME:

BIRTH:

DEATH:

DATE & PLACE OF MARRIAGE:

NAME:

DATE & PLACE OF BIRTH:

DATE & PLACE OF DEATH:

NAME:

BIRTH:

DEATH:

DATE & PLACE OF MARRIAGE:

NAME:

BIRTH:

DEATH:

DATE & PLACE OF MARRIAGE:

NAME:

DATE & PLACE OF BIRTH:

DATE & PLACE OF DEATH:

NAME:

BIRTH:

DEATH:

NAME:

BIRTH:

DEATH:

DATE & PLACE OF MARRIAGE:

NAME:

DATE & PLACE OF BIRTH:

DATE & PLACE OF DEATH:

NAME:

BIRTH:

DEATH:

DATE & PLACE OF MARRIAGE:

NAME:

DATE & PLACE OF MARRIAGE:

NAME:

BIRTH:

DEATH:

NAME:

DATE & PLACE OF BIRTH:

DATE & PLACE OF DEATH:

NAME:

BIRTH:

DEATH:

DATE & PLACE OF MARRIAGE:

NAME:

BIRTH:

DEATH:

ANCESTOR CHARTS

NAME:

DATE & PLACE OF BIRTH:

DATE & PLACE OF DEATH:

PATERNAL GRANDMOTHER
NAME:

DATE & PLACE OF BIRTH:

DATE & PLACE OF MARRIAGE:

DATE & PLACE OF MARRIAGE:

DATE & PLACE OF DEATH:

NAME:

DATE & PLACE OF BIRTH:

DATE & PLACE OF DEATH:

NAME:

BIRTH:

DEATH:

DATE & PLACE OF MARRIAGE:

NAME:

BIRTH:

DEATH:

NAME:

DATE & PLACE OF BIRTH:

DATE & PLACE OF DEATH:

NAME:

BIRTH:

DEATH:

DATE & PLACE OF MARRIAGE:

DATE & PLACE OF MARRIAGE:

NAME:

BIRTH:

DEATH:

NAME:

DATE & PLACE OF BIRTH:

DATE & PLACE OF DEATH:

NAME:

BIRTH:

DEATH:

DATE & PLACE OF MARRIAGE:

NAME:

BIRTH:

DEATH:

NAME:

DATE & PLACE OF BIRTH:

DATE & PLACE OF DEATH:

DATE & PLACE OF MARRIAGE:

NAME:

BIRTH:

DEATH:

NAME:

DATE & PLACE OF MARRIAGE:

NAME:

DATE & PLACE OF BIRTH:

DATE & PLACE OF DEATH:

NAME:

BIRTH:

DEATH:

DATE & PLACE OF MARRIAGE:

NAME:

BIRTH:

DEATH:

ANCESTOR CHARTS

NAME:

DATE & PLACE OF BIRTH:

DATE & PLACE OF DEATH:

MATERNAL GRANDFATHER
NAME:

DATE & PLACE OF BIRTH:

DATE & PLACE OF MARRIAGE:

DATE & PLACE OF DEATH:

DATE & PLACE OF MARRIAGE:

NAME:

DATE & PLACE OF BIRTH:

DATE & PLACE OF DEATH:

NAME:

BIRTH:

DEATH:

DATE & PLACE OF MARRIAGE:

NAME:

DATE & PLACE OF BIRTH:

DATE & PLACE OF DEATH:

NAME:

BIRTH:

DEATH:

DATE & PLACE OF MARRIAGE:

NAME:

BIRTH:

DEATH:

DATE & PLACE OF MARRIAGE:

NAME:

DATE & PLACE OF BIRTH:

DATE & PLACE OF DEATH:

NAME:

BIRTH:

DEATH:

NAME:

BIRTH:

DEATH:

DATE & PLACE OF MARRIAGE:

NAME:

DATE & PLACE OF BIRTH:

DATE & PLACE OF DEATH:

NAME:

BIRTH:

DEATH:

DATE & PLACE OF MARRIAGE:

NAME:

DATE & PLACE OF MARRIAGE:

NAME:

DATE & PLACE OF BIRTH:

DATE & PLACE OF DEATH:

NAME:

BIRTH:

DEATH:

DATE & PLACE OF MARRIAGE:

NAME:

BIRTH:

DEATH:

ANCESTOR CHARTS

NAME:

DATE & PLACE OF BIRTH:

DATE & PLACE OF DEATH:

MATERNAL GRANDMOTHER
NAME:

DATE & PLACE OF BIRTH:

DATE & PLACE OF MARRIAGE:

DATE & PLACE OF DEATH:

DATE & PLACE OF MARRIAGE:

NAME:

DATE & PLACE OF BIRTH:

DATE & PLACE OF DEATH:

NAME:

BIRTH:

DEATH:

DATE & PLACE OF MARRIAGE:

NAME:

BIRTH:

DEATH:

NAME:

DATE & PLACE OF BIRTH:

DATE & PLACE OF DEATH:

NAME:

BIRTH:

DEATH:

DATE & PLACE OF MARRIAGE:

DATE & PLACE OF MARRIAGE:

NAME:

BIRTH:

DEATH:

NAME:

DATE & PLACE OF BIRTH:

DATE & PLACE OF DEATH:

NAME:

BIRTH:

DEATH:

DATE & PLACE OF MARRIAGE:

NAME:

DATE & PLACE OF BIRTH:

DATE & PLACE OF DEATH:

NAME:

BIRTH:

DEATH:

DATE & PLACE OF MARRIAGE:

NAME:

BIRTH:

DEATH:

DATE & PLACE OF MARRIAGE:

NAME:

DATE & PLACE OF BIRTH:

DATE & PLACE OF DEATH:

NAME:

BIRTH:

DEATH:

DATE & PLACE OF MARRIAGE:

NAME:

BIRTH:

DEATH:

FAMILY TREES

Use these pages for any more trees and diagrams you find useful. If you know more generations of ancestors for any branch of your family, you could continue the ancestor charts. Or you could choose to show wider relationships with cousins and other living relatives.

FAMILY TREES

FAMILY TREES

FAMILY TREES

FAMILY PROFILE
MY SPOUSE(S) & CHILDREN

The following profile pages for families and individuals are an opportunity to add more detail than can be shown on a tree or chart. Here, you can record some of your more recent family history.

ME

NAME:

DATE OF BIRTH:

PLACE OF BIRTH:

SPOUSE/PARTNER

NAME:

DATE OF BIRTH:

PLACE OF BIRTH:

DATE AND PLACE OF MARRIAGE:

WHEN AND HOW DID YOU MEET?

WHAT WAS YOUR EARLY LIFE TOGETHER LIKE?

_____

_____

_____

_____

_____

_____

_____

_____

_____

_____

OTHER (THIS COULD INCLUDE PREVIOUS MARRIAGES, STEP-CHILDREN, ETC.):

_____

_____

_____

_____

_____

_____

_____

_____

_____

_____

_____

CHILDREN

NAME	DATE OF BIRTH	PLACE OF BIRTH	SPOUSE/PARTNER & DATE OF MARRIAGE

WHAT ARE YOUR STRONGEST MEMORIES OF YOUR CHILDREN'S CHILDHOODS?

FAMILY PROFILE
MY PARENTS & SIBLINGS

MOTHER

NAME:

FATHER

NAME:

DATE AND PLACE OF MARRIAGE:

HOW DID YOUR PARENTS MEET?

WHAT IS YOUR EARLIEST MEMORY?

WHAT ARE YOUR STRONGEST MEMORIES OF YOUR CHILDHOOD?

SIBLINGS

NAME	DATE OF BIRTH	PLACE OF BIRTH	SPOUSE/PARTNER & DATE OF MARRIAGE

WHAT ARE YOUR STRONGEST MEMORIES OF YOUR SIBLINGS FROM YOUR CHILDHOOD?

_____

_____

_____

_____

_____

_____

_____

_____

_____

_____

_____

_____

_____

_____

PROFILE
MY FATHER

NAME:

NICKNAME(S):

DATE OF BIRTH:

PLACE OF BIRTH:

DATE OF DEATH:

PLACE OF DEATH:

CHILDHOOD AND EDUCATION:

WORK AND INTERESTS:

APPEARANCE:

HEALTH, INCLUDING ILLNESS AND INJURIES:

_____
_____
_____
_____
_____
_____
_____
_____

WHAT ARE YOUR STRONGEST MEMORIES OF YOUR FATHER?

_____
_____
_____
_____
_____
_____
_____
_____

WHAT CHARACTER TRAITS HAVE YOU INHERITED FROM HIM?

_____
_____
_____
_____
_____

PHOTOS

PROFILE
MY MOTHER

NAME:

NICKNAME(S):

DATE OF BIRTH:

PLACE OF BIRTH:

DATE OF DEATH:

PLACE OF DEATH:

CHILDHOOD AND EDUCATION:

WORK AND INTERESTS:

APPEARANCE:

HEALTH, INCLUDING ILLNESS AND INJURIES:

_____

_____

_____

_____

_____

_____

_____

_____

_____

_____

WHAT ARE YOUR STRONGEST MEMORIES OF YOUR MOTHER?

_____

_____

_____

_____

_____

_____

_____

_____

_____

_____

WHAT CHARACTER TRAITS HAVE YOU INHERITED FROM HER?

_____

_____

_____

_____

_____

PHOTOS

FAMILY PROFILE
MY FATHER'S FAMILY

HIS FATHER'S NAME:

HIS MOTHER'S NAME:

PARENTS' DATE AND PLACE OF MARRIAGE:

OTHER NOTES:

THEIR CHILDREN (MY FATHER'S SIBLINGS)

NAME	DATE OF BIRTH	PLACE OF BIRTH	NOTES

FAMILY PROFILE
MY MOTHER'S FAMILY

HER FATHER'S NAME:
_____

HER MOTHER'S NAME:
_____

PARENTS' DATE AND PLACE OF MARRIAGE:
_____
_____

OTHER NOTES:
_____
_____
_____
_____
_____
_____
_____
_____
_____
_____
_____
_____
_____
_____
_____
_____
_____

THEIR CHILDREN (MY MOTHER'S SIBLINGS)

NAME	DATE OF BIRTH	PLACE OF BIRTH	NOTES

PROFILE
MY FATHER'S FATHER

NAME:

NICKNAME(S):

DATE OF BIRTH:

PLACE OF BIRTH:

DATE OF DEATH:

PLACE OF DEATH:

CHILDHOOD AND EDUCATION:

WORK AND INTERESTS:

APPEARANCE:

HEALTH, INCLUDING ILLNESS AND INJURIES:

WHAT ARE YOUR STRONGEST MEMORIES OF YOUR GRANDFATHER? WHAT DID
YOU DO TOGETHER? IF YOU DIDN'T KNOW HIM, WHAT HAVE YOU HEARD ABOUT
HIS CHARACTER?

PROFILE
MY FATHER'S MOTHER

NAME:

NICKNAME(S):

DATE OF BIRTH:

PLACE OF BIRTH:

DATE OF DEATH:

PLACE OF DEATH:

CHILDHOOD AND EDUCATION:

WORK AND INTERESTS:

APPEARANCE:

HEALTH, INCLUDING ILLNESS AND INJURIES:

WHAT ARE YOUR STRONGEST MEMORIES OF YOUR GRANDMOTHER? WHAT DID YOU DO TOGETHER? IF YOU DIDN'T KNOW HER, WHAT HAVE YOU HEARD ABOUT HER CHARACTER?

FAMILY PROFILE
MY FATHER'S GRANDPARENTS

FATHER'S PATERNAL GRANDFATHER

NAME:

DATE AND PLACE OF BIRTH:

DATE AND PLACE OF DEATH:

FATHER'S PATERNAL GRANDMOTHER

NAME:

DATE AND PLACE OF BIRTH:

DATE AND PLACE OF DEATH:

DATE AND PLACE OF MARRIAGE:

WHAT ELSE DO YOU KNOW ABOUT YOUR FATHER'S GRANDPARENTS (YOUR GREAT-GRANDPARENTS) AND YOUR ANCESTORS FURTHER BACK ON YOUR FATHER'S SIDE?

CHILDREN

NAME	DATE OF BIRTH	PLACE OF BIRTH	NOTES

FAMILY PROFILE
MY FATHER'S GRANDPARENTS

FATHER'S MATERNAL GRANDFATHER

NAME:

DATE AND PLACE OF BIRTH:

DATE AND PLACE OF DEATH:

FATHER'S MATERNAL GRANDMOTHER

NAME:

DATE AND PLACE OF BIRTH:

DATE AND PLACE OF DEATH:

DATE AND PLACE OF MARRIAGE:

WHAT ELSE DO YOU KNOW ABOUT YOUR FATHER'S GRANDPARENTS (YOUR GREAT-GRANDPARENTS) AND YOUR ANCESTORS FURTHER BACK ON YOUR FATHER'S SIDE?

CHILDREN

NAME	DATE OF BIRTH	PLACE OF BIRTH	NOTES

PROFILE
MY MOTHER'S FATHER

NAME:

NICKNAME(S):

DATE OF BIRTH:

PLACE OF BIRTH:

DATE OF DEATH:

PLACE OF DEATH:

CHILDHOOD AND EDUCATION:

WORK AND INTERESTS:

APPEARANCE:

HEALTH, INCLUDING ILLNESS AND INJURIES:

WHAT ARE YOUR STRONGEST MEMORIES OF YOUR GRANDFATHER? WHAT DID
YOU DO TOGETHER? IF YOU DIDN'T KNOW HIM, WHAT HAVE YOU HEARD ABOUT
HIS CHARACTER?

PROFILE
MY MOTHER'S MOTHER

NAME:
_____

NICKNAME(S):
_____

DATE OF BIRTH:
_____

PLACE OF BIRTH:
_____

DATE OF DEATH:
_____

PLACE OF DEATH:
_____

CHILDHOOD AND EDUCATION:
_____
_____
_____
_____
_____

WORK AND INTERESTS:
_____
_____
_____
_____
_____

APPEARANCE:
_____
_____
_____
_____
_____

HEALTH, INCLUDING ILLNESS AND INJURIES:

_____

_____

_____

_____

_____

_____

_____

_____

_____

_____

_____

_____

WHAT ARE YOUR STRONGEST MEMORIES OF YOUR GRANDMOTHER? WHAT DID

YOU DO TOGETHER? IF YOU DIDN'T KNOW HER, WHAT HAVE YOU HEARD ABOUT

HER CHARACTER?

_____

_____

_____

_____

_____

_____

_____

_____

FAMILY PROFILE
MY MOTHER'S GRANDPARENTS

MOTHER'S PATERNAL GRANDFATHER

NAME:

DATE AND PLACE OF BIRTH:

DATE AND PLACE OF DEATH:

MOTHER'S PATERNAL GRANDMOTHER

NAME:

DATE AND PLACE OF BIRTH:

DATE AND PLACE OF DEATH:

DATE AND PLACE OF MARRIAGE:

WHAT ELSE DO YOU KNOW ABOUT YOUR MOTHER'S GRANDPARENTS (YOUR GREAT-GRANDPARENTS) AND YOUR ANCESTORS FURTHER BACK ON YOUR MOTHER'S SIDE?

CHILDREN

NAME	DATE OF BIRTH	PLACE OF BIRTH	NOTES

FAMILY PROFILE
MY MOTHER'S GRANDPARENTS

MOTHER'S MATERNAL GRANDFATHER

NAME:

DATE AND PLACE OF BIRTH:

DATE AND PLACE OF DEATH:

MOTHER'S MATERNAL GRANDMOTHER

NAME:

DATE AND PLACE OF BIRTH:

DATE AND PLACE OF DEATH:

DATE AND PLACE OF MARRIAGE:

WHAT ELSE DO YOU KNOW ABOUT YOUR MOTHER'S GRANDPARENTS (YOUR GREAT-GRANDPARENTS) AND YOUR ANCESTORS FURTHER BACK ON YOUR MOTHER'S SIDE?

CHILDREN

NAME	DATE OF BIRTH	PLACE OF BIRTH	NOTES

OTHER ANCESTORS

Use these pages to add information on more distant ancestors, favourite aunts and uncles, or other relatives who achieved great things or who were important in the family. Is there anyone famous or notorious in your family tree?

OTHER ANCESTORS

LIVING RELATIVES

Who are you in touch with who might know more about the family history? Which side are they connected with, and how? Have you spoken to them about the family, or asked them to write in this book?

NAME	DATE OF BIRTH	PARENTS' NAMES

CONTACT DETAILS

NOTES

....
....
....
....
....
....
....
....
....
....
....
....
....
....
....
....
....
....
....

LIVING RELATIVES

NAME	DATE OF BIRTH	PARENTS' NAMES

CONTACT DETAILS

NOTES

....
....
....
....
....
....
....
....
....
....
....
....
....
....
....
....
....
....
....
....
....
....

FAMILY FRIENDS

Close friends can be as important as relatives in a person's life. Who were the most important long-standing friends of your family? How did they come in to the family's life, and what memories do you have of them or what stories have come down to you about them?

FAMILY FRIENDS

STORIES

Are there any stories, jokes or traditions that are passed down in your family? What was a typical family holiday or Christmas like? Do you know of any major historical events your relatives witnessed?

STORIES

STORIES

PLACES

List the places connected with your family. This list could include family homes and favourite holiday destinations. What memories do you have of them? Who lived there? Have you visited or re-visited them? You could use these pages to add information from census and other property records, if you have them.

DATES	PLACE	NOTES

DATES	PLACE	NOTES

PLACES

DATES	PLACE	NOTES

DATES	PLACE	NOTES
....	....	....
....	....	....
....	....	....
....	....	....
....	....	....
....	....	....
....	....	....
....	....	....
....	....	....
....	....	....
....	....	....
....	....	....
....	....	....
....	....	....
....	....	....
....	....	....
....	....	....
....	....	....
....	....	....

To help you research places connected with your family in the past, you can find a wide range of historic maps in local record offices, or online at the National Library of Scotland's website (UK only) or www.oldmapsonline.org.

BURIALS

Memorials to ancestors who have died are important not only as sites for grieving and respect, but also for information. An individual may well have been buried with other family members, and memorials often show dates of birth and other information which can add to the family history.

PERSON	DATE OF DEATH	PLACE OF DEATH	PLACE OF BURIAL/ CREMATION/MEMORIAL, AND INSCRIPTION IF KNOWN
....	....	....	....
....	....	....	....
....	....	....	....
....	....	....	....
....	....	....	....
....	....	....	....
....	....	....	....
....	....	....	....
....	....	....	....
....	....	....	....
....	....	....	....
....	....	....	....
....	....	....	....
....	....	....	....
....	....	....	....
....	....	....	....
....	....	....	....
....	....	....	....

PERSON	DATE OF DEATH	PLACE OF DEATH	PLACE OF BURIAL/ CREMATION/MEMORIAL, AND INSCRIPTION IF KNOWN
....	....	....	....
....	....	....	....
....	....	....	....
....	....	....	....
....	....	....	....
....	....	....	....
....	....	....	....
....	....	....	....
....	....	....	....
....	....	....	....
....	....	....	....
....	....	....	....
....	....	....	....
....	....	....	....
....	....	....	....
....	....	....	....
....	....	....	....
....	....	....	....
....	....	....	....
....	....	....	....
....	....	....	....

WILLS

Many people in the past did not leave wills – but if your ancestors did, they can tell you a range of details on their property, occupations and family members. Do you have copies of wills left by any of your ancestors?

NAME OF DECEASED	DATE OF DEATH	NOTES

NAME OF DECEASED	DATE OF DEATH	NOTES
....	....	....
....	....	....
....	....	....
....	....	....
....	....	....
....	....	....
....	....	....
....	....	....
....	....	....
....	....	....
....	....	....
....	....	....
....	....	....
....	....	....
....	....	....
....	....	....
....	....	....
....	....	....
....	....	....
....	....	....
....	....	....
....	....	....

MIGRATION

When and how did your family move around, either from overseas or within the British Isles? Do you have records of their movements? Do you know what caused them to make the move? Throughout history, people have moved around to find work and better opportunities, as well as to escape hard times or persecution. To find out more about your family's migration between countries, look for documents like naturalization records and ships' passenger lists.

HEIRLOOMS

Documents like family bibles, photo albums, letters and diaries are invaluable for piecing together a family's story. Memorabilia such as jewellery, paintings, furniture or other antiques can also have stories to tell. Do you have, or know of, any special family heirlooms? Where did they come from, and where are they now?

ITEM	WHO DID IT COME FROM?	WHERE IS IT NOW?

ITEM	WHO DID IT COME FROM?	WHERE IS IT NOW?

RELIGION

What role has religion played in your family life? Were there any family members who were particularly religious, or people of different religions? Were your family involved in particular religious communities, churches, temples etc.?

OCCUPATIONS

What sort of work did your ancestors do? Were there any family businesses? Do you know what it was like to work in any of these jobs?

MILITARY SERVICE

Do you know if any of your ancestors served in the military? Which branch of the services were they in? Do you have any official records of their service?

NAME	UNIT(S)	SERVICE NUMBER(S)	ACTIVE SERVICE: CAMPAIGNS, BATTLES OR AWARDS
....	....	....	....
....	....	....	....
....	....	....	....
....	....	....	....
....	....	....	....
....	....	....	....
....	....	....	....
....	....	....	....
....	....	....	....
....	....	....	....
....	....	....	....
....	....	....	....
....	....	....	....
....	....	....	....
....	....	....	....
....	....	....	....
....	....	....	....
....	....	....	....
....	....	....	....

NAME	UNIT(S)	SERVICE NUMBER(S)	ACTIVE SERVICE: CAMPAIGNS, BATTLES OR AWARDS
......	......	......	......
......	......	......	......
......	......	......	......
......	......	......	......
......	......	......	......
......	......	......	......
......	......	......	......
......	......	......	......
......	......	......	......
......	......	......	......
......	......	......	......
......	......	......	......
......	......	......	......
......	......	......	......
......	......	......	......
......	......	......	......
......	......	......	......
......	......	......	......
......	......	......	......
......	......	......	......
......	......	......	......

SECOND WORLD WAR

The Second World War changed the lives of every family in Britain, and many around the world. How did the Second World War affect your family? Do you have any memories of it yourself? Was anyone evacuated? What happened in air raids? Did any of your family do civilian war work?

FIRST WORLD WAR

Though memories of the First World War are more distant, the war affected families hugely. Hundreds of thousands of British servicemen died, and many more came home disabled and traumatised. At home, families coped with rationing and air raids, as well as all the tension of wartime, and women entered new spheres of work in huge numbers. How did the First World War affect your family? Did any of your family do civilian war work?

MYSTERIES

Are there any burning questions you want to answer about your family history?
Have you heard any rumours you would like to prove or disprove?

PHOTOS

Add some of your favourite family photos here, and remember to write down names, places and dates whenever you know them. It's sadly common for families to inherit albums full of anonymous ancestors. Although the contents of your photos may seem obvious to you now, it's worth writing names on the back of as many of your family photos as you can. Printed photos are much easier to preserve for the future than digital files, so remember to print any key images.

PHOTOS

PHOTOS

NOTES

Use these pages to continue your writing from elsewhere in this book, or to make notes on your conversations with family members.

NOTES

NOTES

NOTES

NOTES

NOTES

NOTES

SOURCES

If you have used original documents in your research, including family bibles, wills, certificates of birth, marriage and death, census records, letters and diaries, list them here. Keeping a record of your sources will help you and other researchers to check information and find out more.

SOURCE	YEAR	LOCATION	KEY CONTENTS

SOURCE	YEAR	LOCATION	KEY CONTENTS
....	....	....	....
....	....	....	....
....	....	....	....
....	....	....	....
....	....	....	....
....	....	....	....
....	....	....	....
....	....	....	....
....	....	....	....
....	....	....	....
....	....	....	....
....	....	....	....
....	....	....	....
....	....	....	....
....	....	....	....
....	....	....	....
....	....	....	....
....	....	....	....
....	....	....	....
....	....	....	....
....	....	....	....
....	....	....	....

SOURCES

SOURCE	YEAR	LOCATION	KEY CONTENTS
....	....	....	....
....	....	....	....
....	....	....	....
....	....	....	....
....	....	....	....
....	....	....	....
....	....	....	....
....	....	....	....
....	....	....	....
....	....	....	....
....	....	....	....
....	....	....	....
....	....	....	....
....	....	....	....
....	....	....	....
....	....	....	....
....	....	....	....
....	....	....	....
....	....	....	....
....	....	....	....
....	....	....	....
....	....	....	....

SOURCE	YEAR	LOCATION	KEY CONTENTS
....	....	....	....
....	....	....	....
....	....	....	....
....	....	....	....
....	....	....	....
....	....	....	....
....	....	....	....
....	....	....	....
....	....	....	....
....	....	....	....
....	....	....	....
....	....	....	....
....	....	....	....
....	....	....	....
....	....	....	....
....	....	....	....
....	....	....	....
....	....	....	....
....	....	....	....
....	....	....	....
....	....	....	....
....	....	....	....

MY FAMILY TREE

Use this space to draw out as full a family tree as you can.

TIPS FOR RESEARCH

If this book has inspired you to find out more about your family history, this section will give you some general guidelines for conducting your research. There are endless possibilities for resources to search and techniques to learn. The books and websites referred to here will help to get you started.

There are many different ways to approach your family history research, depending on your goals. You might want to trace your ancestors who share your surname as far back in time as you can, or to collect as many names and dates as possible and draw up an enormous, comprehensive family tree. Or there might be one or two particular questions you feel driven to answer: where in Eastern Europe did your family emigrate from? What did your grandfather do in the war? Is the rumour of an Irish connection true?

If you have a more general interest, you could start by building your family tree until you know the names and dates of all eight of your great-grandparents, or even all sixteen of your great-great-grandparents. You can then work on filling in the details of their lives: their jobs, the places where they lived, their military service, and so on. Be prepared to find that it is simply not possible to 'finish' your family history research. Once you get started, new questions and puzzles will keep on presenting themselves. You may find you have a new hobby for life!

RESEARCH TECHNIQUES

The most important rule of family history research is to START WITH WHAT YOU KNOW, and then work backwards carefully from that. Test and cross-check each new fact you find, especially a link to a new ancestor. This will help you to avoid mistakes, which could send you off down the wrong path and even lead you to research someone else's ancestors.

ASK AROUND to find out if anyone in your family has already done any family history research. There's no need to waste your research time looking for what has already been found. Most families have one or two people who have taken an interest in the family history, or who listened to all the stories. Interview different relatives to get as much information on the various branches of your tree as possible, and also to hear different sides to the story (see pages 148–51 for tips). Remember to ask about the whereabouts of documents and memorabilia. In some families, a box of old papers in the attic can get the lucky family historian started with a wealth of information that would be impossible to find in the archives.

BUILD YOUR TREE, starting with the basics of names, dates and places. If your family was in the UK in the 19th century, you should be able to use the key building blocks of census returns and birth, marriage and death certificates to get your tree back to at least 1841. Civil registration of births, marriages and deaths was introduced in 1837 in England and Wales, and in 1855 in Scotland. The first nationwide census to include individuals' details was taken in England, Wales and Scotland in 1841, and census records are available from then every 10 years until 1911, after which they are closed for privacy and not available to family historians. These records can also reveal details about your ancestors' occupations, homes, illnesses, education and more. The easiest way to access these documents is online, through subscription websites such as Ancestry, Find My Past and The Genealogist. You may be able to access these websites for free at your local library or archive. Once you have used a website to identify a likely birth, marriage or death record from England or Wales in an index, you will need to order copies of the civil registration certificates through the General Record Office for a fee. The official website of the National Records for Scotland, ScotlandsPeople, allows you to view and pay for civil registration records online.

When searching online databases, remember that they often rely on someone having transcribed the handwriting of a family member or an official, and that transcription errors are not uncommon. If you can't find your ancestors, try some lateral thinking: use fuzzy or soundex searches, variations on names, or use fewer search terms – for instance, you may be able to use an ancestor's first name, date and place of birth to search without a surname altogether to find a possible match.

GO FURTHER with different kinds of documents. Once you search beyond census and civil registration records, you can find all sorts of fascinating documents to fill in the stories and bring your ancestors to life. A will could show up unknown relatives, surprising property, or a family grudge; newspaper articles can give a huge amount of detail in an obituary or a report on an accident, or even a trial report with your ancestor's own words recorded. You might find inquest records, apprenticeship records, passenger lists, naturalization records, workhouse and poor law records, personal letters, and all manner of useful sources. Increasing numbers of these kinds of historical documents are available to search and view online.

GET INTO THE ARCHIVES. Despite the huge boom in online genealogy databases and the constant release of newly digitised documents, you will still find plenty of records that are only available in local and specialist archives. Many local record offices and archives are working with the major family history websites to digitise their collections, making more and more of their most popular records searchable online, but this is expensive and labour-intensive, meaning that there is so much more to find that is still undigitised. Local record offices are goldmines for family history, and once you have identified the areas where your ancestors lived, make consulting the local record office there a high priority. Key records held in local record offices include parish registers of baptisms, marriages and burials; maps, including tithe maps which can help you to pinpoint exactly where your ancestors lived around the time of the 1841 census, who their neighbours were, and how much the land was worth; wills; trade directories; land records; and photographs. You may find your research will benefit from visiting one or more of the UK's national archives (the National Archives in Kew, the National Records of Scotland in Edinburgh, or the Public Record Office of Northern Ireland in Belfast), or specialist archives relating to your ancestors' work, ethnicity or other circumstances. Visit in person if you can. Remember to take a camera, as many archives allow you to take your own pictures of documents for a fee; cash is useful, for camera passes or photocopy credits. You should also take a pencil, as pens are usually not allowed in search rooms. If you are unable to travel to the right area, most archives offer a paid research service or a list of freelance researchers who you can hire to do your local research for you. Explore the archive's website and online catalogue first. Above all, talk to the archivists – they are experts on their collections, and will have suggestions for lines of research.

CROSS-REFERENCE and double-check your facts. For each individual and family in your tree, gather as many records as you can. This will help confirm that you have the right people linked to the family, and help you to see and correct any errors or discrepancies in documents. For instance, an individual's age can vary by several years between their marriage certificate, census records and death certificate. People may have had reason to lie about their age, or not have known exactly how old they were, or perhaps the record was filled in by someone else who simply made a mistake. By looking at a range of records you can get an overview of the whole picture. Cross-checking can also stop you from wrongly assuming that a new record you have found belongs to an ancestor of yours. If you find a baptism record that is a likely match with your ancestor, you should check to make sure that there is not a burial record for the same individual a few months later, and whether there are several baptisms with the same name around the same time. Bear in mind that it was common for a family to use several variant spellings of their surname in the past, especially before mass education and literacy took hold in the late 19th century. Another reason for gathering more documents to check against each other is that each extra document just might hold a clue to an exciting new discovery.

NETWORK with other researchers. As well as talking to your known family members, you can also make contact with long-lost relatives, especially online. Many websites, including Ancestry, Genes Reunited, and Jewishgen, have facilities to share your family tree and to connect with other people researching your ancestors. Sharing information with long-lost relatives can lead to great discoveries as well as new friendships. If you find the descendants of your great-uncle who emigrated to America, you might hear a different side to the family story and could find they have documents or photographs of your own ancestors that your side has never seen.

GET THE CONTEXT behind your family story. The bare facts of your family history will come to life when you start researching the historical context. Was your ancestor's death part of a major epidemic? What was it like for footsoldiers to fight alongside your ancestor in the Boer War? What was working life like for your railway-building navvy ancestor? Why did your Jewish ancestors leave eastern Europe when they did? Your family story can lead you into all sorts of fascinating parts of history once you start looking.

HIRE A PROFESSIONAL when you are not able to do the research yourself. If you need to consult documents in an archive which is not convenient for you to travel to, you may want to hire a professional researcher based nearer to the right location. You can find contact details for researchers via local record offices and archives, or on the website of AGRA (the Association of Genealogists & Researchers in Archives) for researchers in the UK, or APG (Association of Professional Genealogists) for researchers worldwide, especially in the USA. You can also find researchers online with a search for 'genealogist' and the location you need. Before you come to an agreement, make sure you're clear on what they are looking for and what kind of records they will search, as well as how much they will charge, how you will pay them, and how long they plan to spend on the research if they charge by the hour. Specify if you want copies of any documents found, and how those will be sent. You will also need to give them as much information as you can on the family or individual they will be researching.

If your family includes ancestors born outside your country of residence, it is even more likely you will need to hire a professional researcher at some point. You should gather as much information as possible on the family members who were born abroad, before you start research in their country of origin. Look for any records which show their date and place of birth, and the names of their parents, siblings and other family members, as well as the details of their journey of immigration. Few countries have centrally-searchable databases with as much coverage as the UK; in many cases, finding out an exact place of origin for your immigrant ancestors will be key to your success.

FURTHER GUIDANCE

- Archives, libraries and adult education centres often run courses or workshops for family history beginners. Check what is available in your area.
- Your local family history society may provide advice and assistance in getting started; or you could join a society based in the area where your ancestors lived, to benefit from that society's research expertise and resources.
- GENUKI is a UK-based website, compiled and maintained by volunteers, which functions as a directory of sources for family history research in the UK and Ireland. It features advice on getting started as well as bibliographies, gazetteers, and information on family history resources at local and national levels. For worldwide research, the website Cyndi's List has a similar function.
- The UK National Archives has a fantastic collection of research guides available on its website, giving general family history advice as well as specific information on how to find documents on topics from adoptions to workhouses.
- There is a wide range of published books on researching your family history, which provide much more advice and information than can be included here. Some useful general guides include:
    - Stella Colwell, *Tracing Your Family History* (Teach Yourself Educational, 2003)
    - Simon Fowler, *Tracing Your Ancestors: A guide for family historians* (Pen and Sword, 2011)
    - David Hey, *The Oxford Guide to Family History* (Oxford University Press, 1993)
    - Mark Herber, *Ancestral Trails: The Complete Guide to British Genealogy and Family History* (Sutton, 1997)

TIPS FOR INTERVIEWING FAMILY MEMBERS

Most of us have questions about our families which we would love to be able to ask certain relatives, if only they were still around. Researching your family history is the perfect prompt to have those sorts of conversations with family members before it's too late. A record of your interviews will be invaluable for you and for researchers in the future, and the experience of sitting down to have a conversation about something you might not often get around to discussing properly can be very worthwhile for both you and your interviewee. Do try to find the time to ask the key questions; you will be glad you did.

WHO AND HOW TO ASK

Try to interview older family members if you can, but don't forget to talk to people of your own generation and even younger too. They may have heard information you haven't, or have a different version of the same family story.

Even people who claim not to know very much can turn out to have valuable memories if you ask the right questions. People with dementia and memory loss often retain interesting memories about their early lives, and can find it enjoyable and beneficial to talk about the past.

Find a time and place where your interviewee is comfortable and you won't be interrupted. Visiting them in their own home is often best.

You may find it easier to split your interview across a number of sessions, if you find you have a lot to talk about. This will also allow you to revisit any gaps in your conversation next time, rather than scrambling to fit everything in in one go.

Record your conversations if possible. You can make notes in this book on the key information, but it will be useful to keep a recording for future reference.

Having a recording will also free you up to listen and take part in the interview, rather than constantly making notes.

Make sure your relative is happy to talk, and understands what you want to do with the information they give you. Let them know whether and how you plan to record and share the interview. If your relative tells you something in confidence which they don't want to be shared further, make sure to honour their wishes. If you find yourself talking about sensitive subjects, watch out for signs of distress; check in with your relative and offer to pause the conversation if they become upset.

Have an idea of the structure of your interview and a list of questions to get you started, but don't feel you have to stick to it too rigidly. If you approach the interview with an open mind, you may make all kinds of unexpected discoveries. You can always fill in unanswered questions or factual gaps at the end of the interview, or another time.

Ask for names, dates and places to fill in your family story, but don't forget that people's less precise memories can be just as useful. A relative might not remember their grandfather's date of death exactly, but may know roughly how old they were when they died, or what time of year it was. They may also know people's nicknames, interests and stories about them which you could never hope to find in official records.

Ask lots of open questions to avoid closing down the answers or putting words in your interviewee's mouth. Practise coming up with questions that start with 'who', 'what', 'where', 'when', 'why' and 'how'. 'What did your grandfather do for a living?' will leave space for a much fuller answer than 'was your grandfather a miner?' You can, of course, use closed questions for checking specific facts and dates.

Try using photographs as a prompt to spark memories. Looking at a wedding photograph can be a fantastic conversation starter: who is in the photo? How are they related? When did the wedding take place? What are they wearing? What did both families think of the match?

Repay your interviewee for their help by sharing what you've found about the family history, as well as asking questions – though not necessarily in the same conversation. The more people feel involved and interested in the process of your research, the more helpful they are likely to be.

WHAT TO ASK

The forms and questions in this book can act as a guide for your conversations. You could take the book with you when you meet, or even lend it to your relatives to get them thinking. Or you could use the prompts in this book to come up with your own list of questions for an interview. For example, if you want to ask about an individual, use one of the individuals' profile pages from this book to remind you to ask about their dates and places of birth, marriage and death, and the names of their spouse and children. You could also ask: did they marry more than once? What did they look like? What was their occupation? Did they serve in the military? Where did they live? Where were they buried? What was their religion?

To give a structure to your conversation, you could work roughly backwards in time down the generations. Start off with your interviewee and ask questions about their own life first. It's useful to start your interview with the basics: ask your relative their full name and any nicknames and maiden names, and their dates and places of birth and marriage, as well as their parents' and siblings' names and dates. If you want to know about your interviewee's life story, then ask questions in order. Start with their birth and childhood, then school and other education, work, and relationships, marriage and parenthood.

If you have time and are interested, your questions can be quite wide-ranging. For instance, you could ask general questions about your relative's childhood and memories of family life. For instance, what was a typical family weekend or Christmas like? What do they remember about their childhood home? Where did they go on holiday? These questions may not be relevant if you only want to find out about more distant family history, but they can preserve precious memories for the future if you do have time to ask.

Once you have talked about your interviewee's own life, ask about their parents. If you are interested in both sides of their family tree, it is less confusing if you deal with them separately. You could start by asking about their father, then about his parents and siblings, and work backwards through the generations on his side before turning to your interviewee's mother's side of the family.

Don't forget to ask if your relatives have any memorabilia, old photos, letters, diaries, or other documents like certificates of birth, marriage or death. Ask whether anyone else has already done research into the family history, and whether you should talk to any other relatives who might know more.

Above all, have fun deepening your connections with your relatives. A family history interview can be an enjoyable process as well as a fact-finding mission.

ABOUT THE AUTHOR

Jo Foster is a writer and family historian. After a History degree at Cambridge University, she worked as a researcher and assistant producer on historical documentaries, including the celebrity family history series *Who Do You Think You Are?*. She has since researched and guided tailor-made family history tours in the UK and Europe with tour company Ancestral Footsteps, as well as writing non-fiction history books and museum guides for children. Jo lives in Winchester with her family. Her ancestors include mill workers, conscientious objectors, and a shipbuilder in Victorian Tyneside who in his spare time was a record-breaking amateur cyclist.

Royal Horticultural Society *My Family Tree*

Published in 2018 by White Lion Publishing, an imprint of The Quarto Group
The Old Brewery, 6 Blundell Street, London, N7 9BH, United Kingdom
www.QuartoKnows.com

Text by Jo Foster
Illustrations © the Royal Horticultural Society and printed under licence granted by the Royal Horticultural Society, Registered Charity number 222879/SC038262

An interest in gardening is all you need to enjoy being a member of the RHS. For more information visit our website rhs.org.uk

A catalogue record for this book is available from the British Library

ISBN 978-0-7112-3989-0

10 9 8 7 6 5 4 3 2

Design by Sarah Pyke

Printed in China